Star of Bethlehem

The Classic QUILT Series #4

LAURA NOWNES

The Quilt Digest Press ∗ *San Francisco*

Editorial and production direction by Michael Kile.
Book editing by Harold Nadel.
Book and cover design by Kajun Graphics.
Quilt photography by Sharon Risedorph and Karen Steffens.
Cover and room setting photographs by Sharon Risedorph.
Computer graphics by Kandy Petersen.
Typographical composition by DC Typography.
Printed by Nissha Printing Company, Ltd., Kyoto, Japan.
Color separations by the printer.
Home graciously lent by Michael and Marion Gates.
Laura is indebted to Joyce Ganser for her help with this technique.

For my Sara, with love.

First Printing.

Library of Congress Cataloging-in-Publication Data

Nownes, Laura, 1953-
    Star of Bethlehem / Laura Nownes.
        p.   cm.
    ISBN 0-913327-25-5 (pbk.) : $6.95
    1. Quilting–Patterns.   I. Title.
TT835.N7   1990
746.9'7–dc20

90-41883
                                                        CIP

The Quilt Digest Press
955 Fourteenth Street
San Francisco 94114

INTRODUCTION

Finding a more dramatic quilt pattern than *Star of Bethlehem* would be a daunting task. Also called *Lone Star,* this pattern has delighted quiltmakers for over a century and a half.

Made challenging by its use of diamond shapes, *Star of Bethlehem* requires careful cutting and piecing to achieve a beautiful quilt. You must be precise to be successful with pieced quilts. My own experience taught me this: I have to be more accurate when working on quilts than I ever had to be as a dress-maker. The ¼″ seam allowance in quiltmaking (as opposed to the ⅝″ seam allowance in dressmaking) allows very little room for error. Some quilt patterns are more forgiving than others. You can often fudge just a bit to compensate for a minor error in cutting or sewing. This is not true with *Star of Bethlehem.* There are many seams, and the accuracy of each angle is critical if the diamonds are to fit together perfectly and allow the finished star to lie flat.

Small errors tend to build as the pieces are joined, and you have one big mess in the end. Worst of all, these errors are not even discovered until too late. They become evident when the last seam, completing the star, is made. Errors will show up as either of two problems at this point: "the beanie effect"—the cen-terpoint sticks up like a beanie instead of lying flat; or the large diamond units ripple instead of lying flat. It is virtually impossible to correct these problems with a finished star.

I am telling you this *not* to discourage you at the outset but to make you aware that these problems will arise if you are not careful, and to let you know there are a few simple but absolutely necessary steps for the success of this quilt:

Always be accurate, every step of the way, cutting and piecing. Double check all of your measurements.

Work slowly. Do not rush through the steps. The results are well worth the extra time and effort.

Press often. Use a good, heavy steam iron, apply-ing pressure. *Do not* push and stretch strips out of shape. They are vulnerable, as their cut edges are all on the bias.

Have fun! This pattern has great sparkle and visual appeal, if you let your creativity guide you.

Read through the general instructions and study the illustrations. When you are ready, choose the quilt you would like to make first. Once you've selected from among the three dramatic quilts presented here, you'll find:

- A full-color photograph of the quilt
- A yardage chart
- Cutting and sewing instructions
- Accurate templates

Making a *Star of Bethlehem* may turn you into a "star" among your family and friends; your creation will be a treasured heirloom for generations to come. Take time to accept and enjoy the admiring com-ments. It's part of the joy of creating a fine *Star of Bethlehem.*

Happy quilting!

Laura

Laura Nownes

WHAT YOU NEED

Fabric—100% cotton—see individual patterns for exact amounts

Thread—100% cotton in a color to blend with your fabrics

Rotary cutter, wide plastic ruler and cutting board -OR- fabric scissors and marking pencil

Glass-head pins

Sewing machine or hand sewing needle

Template plastic (optional)

Black ultra-fine permanent pen (optional)

Paper scissors (optional)

Steam iron

Light-colored towel

Pressing surface

Metal or plastic tape measure

Batting

CUTTING YOUR FABRIC

Look at the "Cutting Your Fabric" chart for the quilt you are working on and cut either the total number of diamonds or total number of strips indicated for each piece of fabric. Yardage is allowed for strips to be cut on the crosswise grain. The charts indicate the template number as well as the width of the strips to cut for each quilt. Use your marking pencil and fabric scissors or rotary cutter, wide plastic ruler and cutting board for this step. Place your cut strips in stacks and label them according to their fabric number.

SEWING STRIPS TOGETHER

Each quilt has a chart showing the order in which fabrics are sewn together for each row of the large diamond unit. If you choose to cut and sew individual diamond shapes together to form the star, then you can simply refer to these charts and sew the shapes in rows. Then join the rows together to make the large diamond units. If you are using the strip piecing method, proceed as follows:

1. Look, for example, at the illustration below:

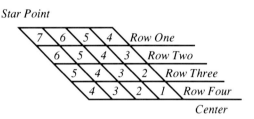

Step 1

Row One consists of one diamond each of fabrics 7, 6, 5 and 4. Row Two consists of one diamond each of fabrics 6, 5, 4 and 3. Row Three consists of one diamond each of fabrics 5, 4, 3 and 2, and Row Four consists of one diamond each of fabrics 4, 3, 2 and 1.

2. To construct Row One, sew the four fabric strips (7, 6, 5 and 4) together lengthwise, as shown in the illustration. Feed the strips evenly through the machine to avoid stretching.

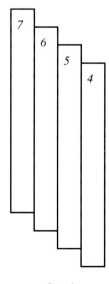

Step 2

Look at the drop between the strips. This is done to prevent wasting fabric when cutting the pieced strips. The distance varies with each pattern.

3. Repeat Step 2 for the fabric strips needed to make Rows Two, Three and Four.

4. Press each seam flat on the wrong side. Then turn the pieced strips to the right side and press the seams in the direction of the strip on the right-hand side of each set. For example, in Row One, press the seams toward fabric strip 4. Make the seams sharp and keep the strips straight.

All three of the patterns in this book require more than four fabric strips per row. I prefer to join 3 or 4 strips at one time and then press. Set these aside, join 3 or 4 more, press and set aside, etc. Then join all sets together to make up the entire row of fabric strips. I find it easier to keep the strips straight by working this way rather than by sewing all 14 or so strips together, then trying to press and keep everything straight.

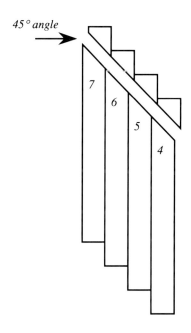

Step 2

CUTTING YOUR PIECED STRIPS

For this next step you can either use a plastic ruler which is marked with a 45-degree angle or make your own template, using the appropriate angle guide for the quilt you are working on (found at the back of the book). Wide plastic rulers and pieces of template plastic are not long enough to extend the full width of the pieced strips. You can cut as far as possible and then slide the ruler, keeping the angle in line to cut the remaining width. Or, you can join only half of the strips required for each row together, cut the pieced strips and then join the two sections together to make the completed row.

1. With the right side facing up, lay the set of Row One pieced strips on a flat surface.

2. Use your plastic ruler or angle guide to achieve the correct angle to mark a line across the pieced strips. Then use your rotary cutter or fabric scissors to cut carefully on the marked line to even off the top jagged edge, as shown in the illustration. An angle guide is given in the back of the book for each quilt. It is helpful in checking the correct angles along the sides of the pieced strips as well as in achieving the exact width of the strips.

3. Use your plastic ruler or angle guide to mark and then cut eight strips from each set, as shown in the illustration. The width of the strips is determined by the quilt you are working on. It should be the same measurement used in cutting your first fabric strips.

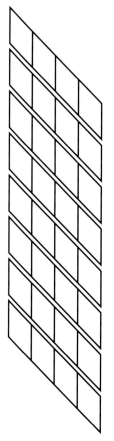

Step 3

This step is critical, as the angle must be exact. You may find after marking and cutting a few strips that your cut angle is no longer in perfect alignment with your angle guide or ruler. You will have to eliminate a small slice from the top edge to get back in line.

4. Place the cut pieced strips in stacks and label them as to their row number. At this point, the cut pieced strips are very fragile and quite susceptible to stretching. Handle them as little as possible. Ideally, store them in a large box or on a board which can be moved to avoid having to disturb them until needed.

5. Repeat Steps 1–4 for the remaining sets of pieced strips.

CONSTRUCTING YOUR LARGE DIAMOND UNITS

1. With their right sides together, sew a Row One pieced strip to a Row Two pieced strip, with a ¼″ seam allowance. This looks tricky at first glance, because the seams are not going in the same direction. In order that the intersections of the diamonds meet, place a pin very close to every seam line in the top strip, ¼″ down from the cut edge. The pin should enter the underlying strip at each corresponding seam line, also ¼″ down from its cut edge. Bring the pin back up and through both layers, at an angle, as shown in the illustration.

Step 1

2. Slowly and carefully sew the cut pieced strips together with a ¼″ seam allowance, removing the pins as you come to them. Let the pieces feed evenly through the machine to avoid stretching.

3. Press the seam flat on the wrong side. Turn to the right side and press the seam toward Row Two. Carefully set aside.

4. Repeat Steps 1–3 for joining Row Three to Row Four.

5. Join the pairs of rows together to form a large diamond unit. Press the new seam flat on the wrong side. Turn to the right side and press it toward Row Four.

6. Repeat Steps 1–5 for the remaining seven large diamond units.

CONSTRUCTING THE STAR

1. Sew large diamond units in pairs, using the technique of pinning through the seams described in Step 1 above. Press the seams *open*.

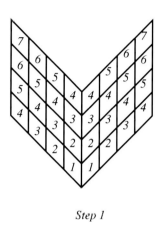

Step 1

2. Pin and then sew pairs together to make two halves of the star. Press these seams *open*.

3. Pin and then sew the two halves together to form the completed star. Press this seam *open*.

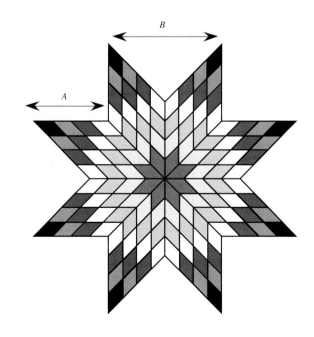

Step 3

At this point I like to lay the star on a flat surface, checking to see that I was careful with all of the steps and that the star lies flat. Use your tape measure to determine the size of the corner squares, as shown by Arrow A in the illustration. Cut four squares of background fabric this size plus approximately an extra inch. The excess will be trimmed off at the end. Next, measure the distance for the side triangles, as shown by Arrow B in the illustration. Add about 2″ to this measurement. Cut one square of background fabric this size. Then cut the square into quarters diagonally to form four triangles.

4. Pin and then inset the corner squares, stitching one side first and then the adjoining side.

5. Pin and then inset the side triangles, stitching one side first and then the adjoining side.

6. Trim off the extra background fabric from around the edges, making sure all sides are the same measurement and that the corners are square.

Steps 4-5

PENNSYLVANIA DUTCH STAR

Maker unknown, c.1890-1910. Collection of Robert and Ardis James.

1⅜″ diamond
Star = 89″

Finished size (approximately)   89″ × 89″

FABRIC NEEDED (YARDS)

Fabric 1: Red (center)

Fabric 2: Navy
Fabric 3: Medium blue
Fabric 4: Light blue
Fabric 5: Gold
Fabric 6: Yellow
Fabric 7: Peach
Fabric 8: Light red
Fabric 9: Medium red
Fabric 10: Light green
Fabric 11: Medium green
Fabric 12: Dark green

Fabrics 2, 3, 5, 6, 7, 10 11 and 12, *each*	⅞
Fabric 4	¼
Fabrics 1, 8 and 9, *each*	1½
Background and binding	3½
Backing	8

CUTTING YOUR FABRIC

Use template A or cut 1½"-wide strips.

Star

Fabrics 1 and 9:

Number of diamonds, *each*	272
-OR- Number of strips, *each*	17

Fabrics 2 and 12:

Number of diamonds, *each*	240
-OR- Number of strips, *each*	15

Fabrics 3 and 11:

Number of diamonds, *each*	248
-OR- Number of strips, *each*	16

Fabric 4:

Number of diamonds	32
-OR- Number of strips	2

Fabrics 5 and 10:

Number of diamonds, *each*	256
-OR- Number of strips, *each*	16

Fabric 6:

Number of diamonds	264
-OR- Number of strips	17

Fabric 7:

Number of diamonds	272
-OR- Number of strips	17

Fabric 8:

Number of diamonds	280
-OR- Number of strips	18

Side and Corner Strips:

Fabrics 1, 8 and 9

Number of 1¾" wide strips, *each*	8

Background: Measure and then *cut when the star is completed.*

Approximate sizes are:

Corner squares: four 23″ squares, *each* cut in half diagonally, and four 4″ squares, *each* cut in half diagonally.

Side triangles: one 30″ square, cut into quarters diagonally, and two 7½″ squares cut into quarters diagonally.

Backing: number of lengths 3

PUTTING IT ALL TOGETHER

1. Set aside the 8 strips each from fabrics 1, 8 and 9 for the side and corner strips on the background pieces.

2. Cut all of the remaining strips in half to make pieces 1½″ × approximately 22″ (as fabric widths vary).

3. The fabric strip combinations for each row are as follows:

Row One:	3-2-12-11-10-1-9-8-7-6-5-3-2-12-11-10-1-9-8
Row Two:	2-12-11-10-1-9-8-7-6-5-3-2-12-11-10-1-9-8-7
Row Three:	12-11-10-1-9-8-7-6-5-3-2-12-11-10-1-9-8-7-6
Row Four:	11-10-1-9-8-7-6-5-3-2-12-11-10-1-9-8-7-6-5
Row Five:	10-1-9-8-7-6-5-3-2-12-11-10-1-9-8-7-6-5-3
Row Six:	1-9-8-7-6-5-3-2-12-11-10-1-9-8-7-6-5-3-2
Row Seven:	9-8-7-6-5-3-2-12-11-10-1-9-8-7-6-5-3-2-12
Row Eight:	8-7-6-5-3-2-12-11-10-1-9-8-7-6-5-3-2-12-11
Row Nine:	7-6-5-3-2-12-11-10-1-9-8-7-6-5-3-2-12-11-10
Row Ten:	6-5-3-2-12-11-10-1-9-8-7-6-5-3-2-12-11-10-1
Row Eleven:	5-3-2-12-11-10-1-9-8-7-6-5-3-2-12-11-10-1-9
Row Twelve:	3-2-12-11-10-1-9-8-7-6-5-3-2-12-11-10-1-9-8
Row Thirteen:	2-12-11-10-1-9-8-7-6-5-3-2-12-11-10-1-9-8-7
Row Fourteen:	12-11-10-1-9-8-7-6-5-3-2-12-11-10-1-9-8-7-6
Row Fifteen:	11-10-1-9-8-7-6-5-3-2-12-11-10-1-9-8-7-6-5
Row Sixteen:	10-1-9-8-7-6-5-3-2-12-11-10-1-9-8-7-6-5-4
Row Seventeen:	1-9-8-7-6-5-3-2-12-11-10-1-9-8-7-6-5-4-3
Row Eighteen:	9-8-7-6-5-3-2-12-11-10-1-9-8-7-6-5-4-3-2
Row Nineteen:	8-7-6-5-3-2-12-11-10-1-9-8-7-6-5-4-3-2-1

4. Sew the fabric strips together for each row in the order given in Step 3. The drop between strips is 1″.

5. Mark and then cut eight 1½″-wide pieced strips from each set, using either a template of the angle guide for the Pennsylvania Dutch Star found in the back of the book or a wide plastic ruler marked with a 45-degree angle. See Step 2 in "Cutting Your Pieced Strips" in the general instructions for help.

6. Join the pieced strips to make eight large diamond units.

7. Join the large diamond units to make a completed star.

8. Sew the 1¾″-wide strips of fabrics 1, 8 and 9 together for joining to the background pieces.

9. Lay the star out onto a flat surface. Place the pieced strips around the edges of the star to determine the required lengths. The approximate length of the strips for the corner square is 30½″ and the approximate length of the strips for the side triangle is 27″. Trim to fit, remembering to add seam allowance.

10. Attach the small triangles of background fabric to each pieced strip, as shown in the illustrations.

11. Join the background pieces to the pieced strips, as shown in the illustrations. Trim any excess as necessary.

12. Inset the corner squares and side triangles into the star.

13. Your quilt top is now ready to be layered and hand or machine quilted.

14. Finish the edges with a ¼″ binding.

For corner squares

For side triangles

Step 10

Corner square

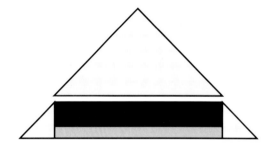

Side triangle

Step 11

STAR CONSTELLATION

Maker unknown, c.1840. Collection of Robert and Ardis James.

2⅜″ diamonds
Main star = 113¾″
Corner stars = 24⅜″

Finished size (approximately)   130″ × 130″

If you would like to make a smaller quilt, you can use template
A (or cut 1½″-wide strips) to make a finished quilt of 76″ × 76″.

FABRIC NEEDED (YARDS)

Fabric 1: Brown (center)	**Fabric 1**	2½
Fabric 2: Red	**Fabric 2**	2¾
Fabric 3: Gold	**Fabric 3**	3⅜
Fabric 4: Teal	**Fabric 4**	1¾
Fabric 5: Beige	**Fabric 5**	¾
Fabric 6: Pink	**Fabric 6**	1¾
Fabric 7: Burgundy	**Fabric 7**	⅞
Fabric 8: Light blue	**Fabric 8**	½
Fabric 9: Tan	**Fabric 9**	⅜
	Background	3½
	Border	3¾
	Backing	11¼
	Binding	1

CUTTING YOUR FABRIC

Use template B or cut 2⅛″-wide strips.

Fabric 1
Number of diamonds	312
-*OR*- Number of strips	39

Fabric 2
Number of diamonds	368
-*OR*- Number of strips	46

Fabric 3
Number of diamonds	424
-*OR*- Number of strips	53

Fabric 4
Number of diamonds	216
-*OR*- Number of strips	27

Fabric 5
Number of diamonds	72
-*OR*- Number of strips	9

Fabric 6
Number of diamonds	224
-*OR*- Number of strips	28

Fabric 7
Number of diamonds	80
-*OR*- Number of strips	10

Fabric 8
Number of diamonds	40
-*OR*- Number of strips	5

Fabric 9
Number of diamonds	24
-*OR*- Number of strips	3

Background: Measure and then *cut when star is completed.*

Approximate sizes are: twenty 12″ squares; two 18½″ squares, *each* cut into quarters diagonally; and two 16½″ squares, *each* cut into quarters diagonally.

Border: width	8½″
Backing: number of lengths	3

PUTTING IT ALL TOGETHER

1. The fabric strip combinations for each row of the main star are as follows:

Row One:	1-5-9-2-8-3-1-2-4-7-3-6-1-2
Row Two:	5-9-2-8-3-1 2-4-7-3-6-1-2-3
Row Three:	9-2-8-3-1-2-4-7-3-6-1-2-3-4
Row Four:	2-8-3-1-2-4-7-3-6-1-2-3-4-1
Row Five:	8-3-1-2-4-7-3-6-1-2-3-4-1-6
Row Six:	3-1-2-4-7-3-6-1-2-3-4-1-6-3
Row Seven:	1-2-4-7-3-6-1-2-3-4-1-6-3-2
Row Eight:	2-4-7-3-6-1-2-3-4-1-6-3-2-5
Row Nine:	4-7-3-6-1-2-3-4-1-6-3-2-5-4
Row Ten:	7-3-6-1-2-3-4-1-6-3-2-5-4-3
Row Eleven:	3-6-1-2-3-4-1-6-3-2-5-4-3-2
Row Twelve:	6-1-2-3-4-1-6-3-2-5-4-3-2-3
Row Thirteen:	1-2-3-4-1-6-3-2-5-4-3-2-3-2
Row Fourteen:	2-3-4-1-6-3-2-5-4-3-2-3-2-1

2. Sew the strips together for each row in the order given in Step 1. The drop between the strips is 1⅝″.

3. Mark and then cut eight 2⅛″-wide pieced strips from each set, using either a template of the angle guide for the main star found in the back of the book or a wide plastic ruler marked with a 45-degree angle. See Step 2 in "Cutting Your Pieced Strips" in the general instructions for help.

4. Join the pieced strips to make eight large diamond units.

5. Join the large diamond units to make a completed star.

6. The fabric strip combinations for each row of the small stars are as follows. Make six combinations of *each* row.

Row One:	1-3-2
Row Two:	3-2-6
Row Three:	2-6-1

7. Sew the strips together for each row of the small stars in the order given in Step 6. The drop between the strips is 1⅝″.

8. Mark and then cut eight 2⅛″-wide pieced strips from each set, either making a template of the angle guide for the small stars found in the back of the book or using a wide plastic ruler marked with a 45-degree angle.

9. Join the pieced strips to make large diamond units. You will need 48.

10. Join the large diamond units to make four whole stars and four half stars.

11. Measure and check to see that the approximate sizes for the background fabric given above in the cutting chart are large enough for your small completed stars. They need to be generous to fit into the sides and corners of the main star.

12. Inset the corner squares and side triangle pieces into the small stars, trimming the excess length from the side triangles, as shown in the illustration.

13. Even off the edges of these finished pieces. Then inset them into the main star, trimming excess as needed.

14. Attach the border strips.

15. Your quilt top is now ready to be layered and hand or machine quilted.

16. Finish the edges with a ¼″ binding.

Star Constellation
Step 12

Amish maker unknown, c.1920. The Esprit Quilt Collection, San Francisco.

2½″ diamond

Star = 60″

Finished size (approximately)　　90″ × 90″

If you would like to make a smaller quilt, use template A (or cut
1½″ wide strips) to make a finished quilt 62″ × 62″.

FABRIC NEEDED (YARDS)

Fabric 1: White (center)	**Fabrics 1 and 13,** *each*	⅛
Fabric 2: Red	**Fabrics 2, 3, 11 and 12,** *each*	¼
Fabric 3: Black	**Fabrics 4 and 10,** *each*	⅜
Fabric 4: Pink	**Fabrics 5, 6, 8 and 9,** *each*	½
Fabric 5: Teal	**Fabric 7**	⅝
Fabric 6: Lavender	**Background**	2
Fabric 7: Muddy green	**Border**	2⅝
Fabric 8: Plum	**Binding**	2⅝
Fabric 9: Bright pink	**Backing**	8
Fabric 10: Navy		
Fabric 11: Gold		
Fabric 12: Green		
Fabric 13: Dark plum		

CUTTING YOUR FABRIC

Use template C or cut 2¼" wide strips.

Fabrics 1 and 13:

Numbers of diamonds, *each*	8
-or- Number of strips, *each*	1

Fabrics 2 and 12:

Numbers of diamonds, *each*	16
-or- Number of strips, *each*	2

Fabrics 3 and 11:

Numbers of diamonds, *each*	24
-or- Number of strips, *each*	3

Fabrics 4 and 10:

Numbers of diamonds, *each*	32
-or- Number of strips, *each*	4

Fabrics 5 and 9:

Numbers of diamonds, *each*	40
-or- Number of strips, *each*	5

Fabrics 6 and 8:

Numbers of diamonds, *each*	48
-or- Number of strips, *each*	6

Fabric 7:

Number of diamonds	56
-or- Number of strips	7
Border: width	13½"
Backing: number of lengths	3
Background:	Measure and then *cut when star is completed.*
Approximate sizes are: Corner square:	four 18½" squares
Side triangles:	one 28" square cut into quarters diagonally.

PUTTING IT ALL TOGETHER

1. The fabric strip combinations for each row are as follows:

Row One:	13-12-11-10-9-8-7
Row Two:	12-11-10-9-8-7-6
Row Three:	11-10-9-8-7-6-5

Row Four:	10-9-8-7-6-5-4
Row Five:	9-8-7-6-5-4-3
Row Six:	8-7-6-5-4-3-2
Row Seven:	7-6-5-4-3-2-1

2. Sew the strips together for each row in the order given in Step 1. The drop between the strips is 1¾".

3. Mark and then cut eight 2¼"-wide pieced strips from each set, using either a template of the angle guide for the Amish Star found in the back of the book or a wide plastic ruler marked with a 45-degree angle. See Step 2 in "Cutting Your Pieced Strips" in the general instructions for help.

4. Join the pieced strips to make eight large diamond units.

5. Join the large diamond units to make a completed star.

6. Measure and then cut the corner squares and side triangles from the background fabric.

7. Inset the background pieces.

8. Attach the border strips.

9. Your quilt top is now ready to be layered and hand or machine quilted.

10. Attach the binding. The finished width is 1¾".

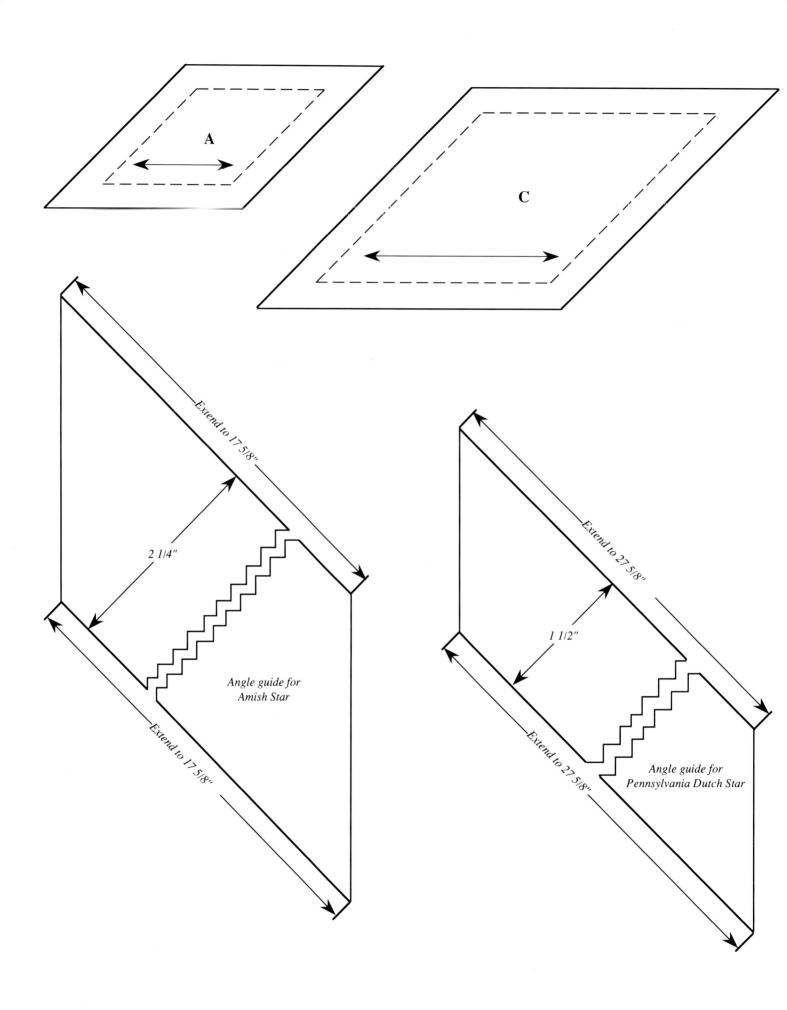

A

C

Extend to 17 5/8"

2 1/4"

Angle guide for
Amish Star

Extend to 17 5/8"

Extend to 27 5/8"

1 1/2"

Extend to 27 5/8"

Angle guide for
Pennsylvania Dutch Star

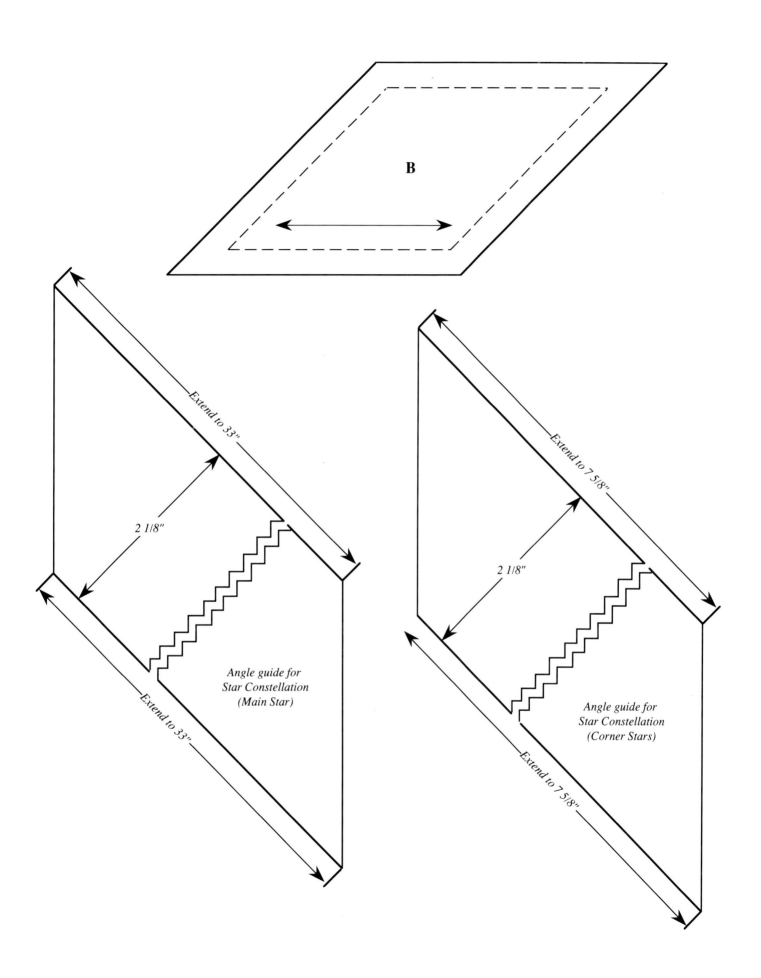

B

Extend to 33"

2 1/8"

Extend to 33"

*Angle guide for
Star Constellation
(Main Star)*

Extend to 7 5/8"

2 1/8"

Extend to 7 5/8"

*Angle guide for
Star Constellation
(Corner Stars)*

Simply the Best

*W*hen we started our publishing efforts in 1983, we made one pledge to ourselves: to produce the finest quilt books imaginable. The critics and our loyal readers clearly believe that we're living up to that promise.

In a time when thin, 64-page quilt books with only staples to hold their pages intact and small numbers of color photos sell for as much as $19.95, we are proud that our books set a noticeably higher standard.

Books from The Quilt Digest Press are hefty, with many more pages and masses of color photos. They are printed on high-quality satin-finish paper and are bound with durable glues and spines to last a lifetime. The world's finest quilt photographer does all our work. A great design team lavishes its attention on every detail of every page. And the world's finest commercial printer sees to it that every book is a gem. Add knowledgeable authors with vital ideas and you, too, will say, "The Quilt Digest Press? Oh, they're Simply the Best."

Try another of our books. They're as good as the one in your hands. And write for our free color catalogue.

THE QUILT DIGEST PRESS

Dept. D
955 Fourteenth Street
San Francisco 94114